Original title:
Tying the Dreams

Copyright © 2025 Creative Arts Management OÜ
All rights reserved.

Author: Dorian Ashford
ISBN HARDBACK: 978-1-80586-165-2
ISBN PAPERBACK: 978-1-80586-637-4

Embracing Boundless Possibilities

In the land where wishes roam,
A chicken dreams of flying home.
With googly eyes and flapping wings,
It gathers strength, and boldly sings.

A fish in boots rides on a bike,
Chasing clouds, avoiding a strike.
It winks at stars with silly grace,
While jellybeans dance in outer space.

Intricate Weaves of Forgotten Dreams

A spider spun a web of thought,
With dandelions, battles fought.
Each thread a tale of yesteryear,
Where socks find mates, and frogs hold beer.

Lost socks gather for a parade,
In mismatched shoes, they're unafraid.
With laughter loud, they take on fate,
An epic quest to find their mate.

Veils of the Mind's Canvas

A painter smeared a cloud with glee,
While tickled brushes danced like bees.
The colors giggled, splashed about,
As paint tubes whispered tales, no doubt.

A canvas turned and waved hello,
To all the dreams that long to grow.
They juggled wishes, laughter bright,
In a carnival of pure delight.

The Chord of Yearnings

A guitar strummed a silly tune,
While dreams bounced 'round like a cartoon.
They tickled strings and started to hum,
A melody where nonsense came from.

With ukuleles in dancing hands,
They formed a band on wobbly stands.
Each note a giggle, light and free,
As rhythms played with jubilee.

The Knotting of Souls

Messy yarns will twine around,
Catch your laughter as it bounds.
A playful tug, a silly spin,
We dance together, let's begin.

With socks and hats, a knitted spree,
We'll stitch our tales with glee, you see!
A tangled mess, a laughter spree,
Life's little knots, just you and me.

Tapestry of Yearning

Threads of hope in colors bright,
We'll weave them through the day and night.
Woolly whims and silly schemes,
In every stitch, we find our dreams.

A patchwork quilt, so grand and bold,
With pockets full of tales untold.
We'll fancy colors with a twist,
In every loop, a giggle kissed.

United in Reverie

Floating high on dreams afresh,
A trampoline of thoughts enmesh.
With every bounce, the sky we meet,
Laughter echoes, oh what a treat!

In fairytale tinfoil hats we wear,
We'll leap and dance without a care.
Flying high on whims and giggles,
United in jests, our joy just wiggles.

Medley of Dreams

Like spaghetti noodles on the floor,
Our hopes collide, what's in store?
We stir and twirl this silly pot,
With each new mix, we find a lot.

Cotton candy clouds in the air,
Swinging high without a care.
A blend of wishes, bright and sweet,
In this mad medley, we find our beat.

Connections in a Starry Fabric

Under the stars, we weave our plots,
With glitter and giggles, we tie our knots.
A cat in a hat joins in our play,
Dancing on clouds while we dream away.

Jellybeans roll in the cosmic breeze,
As we float on laughter, feeling at ease.
UFOs giggle at our silly schemes,
Crafting new worlds from whimsical dreams.

The Fabric of Midnight Hopes

In the quiet of night, we stitch our goals,
With threads of mischief, and colorful trolls.
A wink from the moon, a grin from the sun,
Gathered together, oh what fun!

Boys in pajamas chase fireflies,
While girls in tiaras plan midnight pies.
A recipe for laughter, a sprinkle of light,
In this fabric of hopes, everything's bright.

Binding Fantasies in Silent Starlight

Under the blanket of twinkling stars,
We bind our whims with candy bars.
Wizards in sneakers, dragons in shirts,
Creating wild tales where silliness flirts.

A tangle of wishes, a jumble of fun,
As we skip through dreams, each laugh weighs a ton.
With each silly dance and each twist of fate,
We laugh at the cosmos, it's never too late.

Weaving the Threads of Tomorrow

With a spool of giggles, we craft our day,
Knitting together the plans in a playful way.
A squirrel in a tie sells tickets to dreams,
While penguins in bowties join in the schemes.

The future is bright as we prank the dawn,
With tutus and capes, we all put our brawn.
A carnival ride through the fields of today,
Unraveling laughter along the way.

The Tangle of Wishes

In the backyard, wishes grow,
Like tangled vines, don't you know?
A squirrel stole one for his lunch,
While I just laugh, a little hunch.

A kite got caught on a tree branch,
Floating dreams in a silly dance.
The sun, it smirks as they collide,
With laughter echoing, wide-eyed.

Ensnared in Hope

Hope is a cat with too much yarn,
Twisting and turning, oh so far.
Chasing shadows in a playful chase,
Laughter erupts; it's a merry place.

My wishes fly like paper planes,
Loop-de-looping through silly stains.
The dog barks loud, he joins the fun,
A circus act beneath the sun!

Cloaked in Fantasy

A wizard's hat on a scarecrow's head,
Casting spells that tickle instead.
With giggles, gnomes leap from their spots,
In a jumble of laughter, a world that knots.

Fairy wings made of buttercup,
Whirling around, never give up.
Frogs in tuxedos spin and sway,
As fantasy giggles the day away.

The Narrative of Threads

Threads of stories, a funny weave,
Knots of comedy, take a leave.
Jumping beans in a jolly fuss,
While socks tell tales without a fuss.

Each stitch a tickle, each loop a cheer,
Laughing together, while sipping beer.
In this tapestry of silly schemes,
A patchwork quilt full of quirky dreams.

Mended Yearnings

In a world that spins so wide,
I chase my hopes with joyful pride.
A sock and shoe, both mismatched,
Life's little quirks are quite attached.

The moon wore shades on a sunny day,
While frogs in tuxedos danced away.
With kite tails tangled in the trees,
I giggle at the silliest of these.

Patchwork of Possibilities

A quilt of dreams, with patches bright,
Stitched together in pure delight.
A cat in boots, a dog in furs,
Reality is just absurd.

I sip my tea, a circus clown,
With jelly beans to wear as crowns.
The sun plays peekaboo, oh my!
While rainbows dance and seagulls fly!

Swirling Threads of Fate

My life's a tapestry of fun,
With every thread, a joke to run.
A dragon flies with pizza wings,
And laughter joyfully springs.

The universe does cartwheels bright,
As jellyfish glow in the night.
With every twist the cosmos makes,
The silly joy of dreams awakes.

Endless Possibility

When marshmallows grow on trees,
I build a house that sways and frees.
A slide from clouds into the blue,
Where giggles burst like bubbles too.

The butterfly grins, it's quite absurd,
As unicorns slide without a word.
On a trampoline of dreams so fair,
I bounce into the endless air.

Colorful Hues of Hopeful Schemes

In a land where rainbows sprout,
Chasing wishes, roundabout.
A polka-dotted unicorn,
Wears a hat that's slightly worn.

With jellybeans for morning tea,
And dancing ants as company.
On a trampoline made of cheese,
We bounce our dreams with perfect ease.

Twisted Vines of Ambition

A twisty vine climbs up the wall,
Wearing socks that squeak and call.
It dreams of grapes but gets a shoe,
With laces tied in knots of blue.

A daisy dons a polka dot,
In fields where every dream is hot.
It sways and sings a silly tune,
Under the light of a smiling moon.

Glimmers at Twilight's Edge

At dusk, the stars begin to wink,
While turtles wear a bow on pink.
They launch their boats of paper skies,
And sail through clouds with silly sighs.

A firefly sparkles doing flips,
Chasing dreams from sunny trips.
With every buzz, a giggle bursts,
In twilight's glow where fun resides first.

The Stitch of Serendipity

In Grandma's quilt, a tale is sown,
With stitching laughter, brightly shown.
A cat in mittens rides a train,
While juggling jelly, what a gain!

A patchwork dream drapes all around,
With giggles bouncing, joy is found.
So let's chase fun, not take a nap,
With quirky dreams in every flap.

Fates Intertwined

In a world of mismatched socks,
Dreamers meet with wily clocks.
One thinks of cheese, the other, cake,
Together they plot for a jester's shake.

With a hat made of feathers, bright and bold,
They giggle at stories yet to be told.
Their plans are silly, a chaotic swirl,
As they dance through life in a dizzy whirl.

Ribbons of Imagination

Bright ribbons flutter in the sun,
Each twist and turn is silly fun.
One's a dragon, the other's a cat,
Playing hopscotch with a teddy bat.

They sketch their worlds in ice cream cones,
With castles built of jellybeans and scones.
Laughter echoes through their fun-filled scheme,
Two goofs creating their favorite dream.

The Dreamer's Tapestry

Stitch by stitch, they weave their fates,
With silly patterns made from plates.
A hammock swings where giggles soar,
And unicorns dance on a candy store.

Swirling colors, a laugh, a shout,
They throw in sprinklers just to sprout.
Their silly fabric, bright and loud,
Makes even grumpy cats feel proud.

Dance of Ambitions

With a hop and a skip, they take the stage,
Dreams pirouette, wild like a mage.
One wants to fly, the other, to bake,
Sprinkling laughter with each little break.

They tango with squirrels, waltz with the moon,
While singing to ducks in an old cartoon.
Their ambitions spark like fireworks bright,
Silliness shines, like stars in the night.

Cultivating a Garden of Fancies

In a plot where whims can bloom,
I planted seeds of laugh and gloom.
The daisies giggle, the roses dance,
While carrots plot their escape chance.

Butterflies sipping on sweet delight,
Chasing shadows in playful flight.
A gnome in the corner starts to sing,
As mushrooms wear hats, a quirky thing.

The sun throws a party, the clouds bring cheese,
While daisies wink with the greatest ease.
We chase our tails in this vibrant patch,
With bumblebees buzzing—what a catch!

So come join the fun, let's weed out frowns,
In this garden, there are no sad clowns.
Digging up laughter, planting a smile,
In the soil of nonsense, we'll play for a while.

Braided Journeys through Sleep

In a land where snuggles weave,
My pillow whispers, 'Come believe!'
With dreams that twirl on candy trails,
And teddy bears dressed as whales.

I ride on unicorns in pajamas bright,
Through cotton candy clouds at night.
But watch out for the marshmallow tide,
It's slippery, oh, what a wild ride!

I meet a snail wearing a bow tie,
Sipping tea with the moon in the sky.
We trade tall tales with a rubber duck,
And share our dreams with a dash of luck.

The sun peeks in, "Is naptime done?"
The dreamlike giggles, oh what fun!
As we wake with smiles, don't lose the thread,
Of those wild adventures where we both fled.

A Quilt of Wandering Thoughts

In a patchwork of ideas, so bright,
I stitched together bits of delight.
A square for worries, a hex for cheer,
Tangled threads whisper, 'Come here!'

Each piece a memory, a quirky line,
Mixed with snippets of punch and wine.
The seams of laughter, quilted tight,
Keep the chills of boredom out of sight.

With buttons of giggles and patches of fun,
This quilt wraps round, each thought a pun.
A cozy embrace in a chaotic spree,
Where all can come, come sit with me!

So grab a cup of whimsical tea,
With every sip, dream's jubilee.
In this quilt of thoughts, let's weave and twine,
Embrace the nonsense and feel divine.

In the Loom of Infinity

In an endless loom, we weave our play,
Silly strands twist and twirl as they sway.
Each loop tells a tale of giggling glee,
As we dance around the wild bumblebee.

Oh, look there! A sock has slipped away,
It's off on adventures, come what may!
With mismatched shoes running in a race,
Who knew that fashion could be such a space?

Threads of imagination, stretchy and bright,
Colorful chaos—a comical sight.
We chuckle and weave, letting whimsy flow,
In this fabric of time where oddities glow.

So spin your yarns, let them unfold,
In the loom of mishaps, be daring, be bold.
For in the tapestry of mirth we'll find,
That laughter's the thread that ties us all blind!

Whirling Dreams

In a toaster, I found my fate,
Pancakes dancing, what a state!
A cat on a skateboard, quite a sight,
Chasing the moon, oh what a night!

Jellybeans rain from the skies,
Floating like clouds, oh what a surprise!
A chicken in a top hat, bold and grand,
Doing the cha-cha, ain't life just grand?

A llama with glasses, reading a book,
In a library nook, come take a look!
With a hat made of cheese and socks made of fries,
Who knew daydreams could be such a prize?

So may your thoughts spin, twirl, and glide,
Embrace the silly, laughter your guide!
We'll gather the giggles, a peculiar team,
Chasing the joyous, in wacky dreams!

Intwined Journeys

A rubber chicken, off on a spree,
With a bouncy ball, they fly like a bee!
The bus is a dragon, with wheels made of gum,
Puffing along, here it comes!

Jumping on clouds, in socks two sizes too big,
A polar bear twirls, teaching a jig!
A pushpin parade, marching in line,
While unicorns sip on fizzy grape wine!

Explorers in slippers, they wander and slide,
Through a world made of jelly, they giggle with pride!
With mischievous squirrels keeping the score,
Every twist and turn opens new doors!

So let's pack our laughter, no time to waste,
With whimsy our guide, oh what a taste!
As we wander through giggles, the fun never ends,
In this merry journey, joyfully blend!

Time's Tapestry

A clock made of cheese, ticking away,
And every hour brings a comical play!
With squirrels as conductors, music quite grand,
They lead a parade of cupcakes on hand!

Sprinkles rain down like confetti of cheer,
Each tick of the hand brings silly near!
With jellyfish knitting in colors so bright,
They weave all our laughter into the night!

Time takes a break, laughs with delight,
In a circus of bubbles, floating in flight!
While teacups and saucers dance round and round,
In this whimsical world, joy can be found!

So let the hours giggle and play,
In their own special, quirky way!
For in this grand tapestry, we will find,
Every moment's a treasure, silly and kind!

The Synthesis of Being

In the lab of giggles, we mix and we blend,
With giggle juice bottles, our laughter won't end!
Twirling and whirling, concocting delight,
With bubblegum theories taking their flight!

A penguin in glasses pens poems with flair,
While dancing with flamingos without a care!
They holler and cackle, creation's delight,
As dreams waltz together, oh what a sight!

With marshmallow thoughts and chocolate ideas,
They bubble with laughter, let go of their fears!
In this merry mixer, we'll throw in some fun,
Stirred with a giggle, we shine like the sun!

So join in the chaos, embrace every scheme,
For life is a potion, infused with our dream!
With each playful moment, life's essence is spun,
In this fabulous fusion, let the fun run!

Reverberating Aspirations

A goat in a hat sings with glee,
While visions of grandeur dance by a tree.
A pizza delivery on a jet ski,
Who knew dreams could be so cheesy?

Rainclouds dress in polka dots bright,
As balloons float off into the night.
Juggling jellybeans, oh what a sight,
These wacky ideas take flight with delight!

Chronicles of Creation

A wizard forgot where he placed his wand,
Accidentally turning his frog into fond.
Magic spilled everywhere, quite despond,
Even the cauldron has now got a bond!

A sandwich that sings, what a delight,
Crooning ballads under the moonlight.
Peanut butter and jelly in a twirl so tight,
Creating a sandwich with purest of might!

The Essence of Union

Two socks joined hands in a dance so fine,
Who knew laundry could lead to romance divine?
The left sock sighed, 'You're simply divine!'
As they tangoed past the bottle of brine!

A cat and a fish share an ice cream cone,
While dreaming of travel far from their home.
In a world where cats and fish freely roam,
They sip on the whims of a gelato foam!

Frayed Edges

A piece of fabric with stories to tell,
Woven with laughter, a patchwork of swell.
It frayed at the edges, but oh how it fell,
A tapestry spinning a whimsical spell!

Kites in the breeze, shaped like a shoe,
Only to crash into grandma's stew.
With giggles and wiggles, the chaos ensues,
A dinner of laughter, who knew it was due?

The Alchemy of Ascent

In a world where wishes float,
A penguin dreams to sail a boat.
He waves his flippers, starts to bake,
But ends up with a giant cake.

With frosting waves and cherry sails,
He lifts off with his fishyails.
The seagulls cheer, the crabs all grin,
This pastry pirate's bound to win!

Fastened by Vision

A squirrel with goggles, perched up high,
Dreams of flying through the sky.
With acorns packed in his small pack,
He hops in a balloon—then goes whack!

He drifts past clouds, makes friends with bees,
And shouts, "I'm off to find some cheese!"
But mid-air, he drops a nutty snack,
And lands, confused, on a grumpy cat's back!

The Manifestation Mosaic

Building castles out of cheese,
A mouse yells, "Oh, what a tease!"
He throws the bits, sticks on some glue,
And soon has guests—both old and new.

With cheddar bricks and Swiss-built doors,
They dance and laugh on cheese-smelling floors.
But when the cat comes to the feast,
They hide and squeak—oh what a beast!

Loops of Imagination

A frog in a top hat loves to sing,
And dreams of owning a tiny fling.
He hops on lily pads, leaps for joy,
Singing, "I want a magic toy!"

But when he wished on a shooting star,
A rubber duck flew from afar.
Now every night is quite a quack,
As frogs and ducks have a party to stack!

Handcrafted Aspirations

In my attic, a squirrel stashed,
Dreams in corners, all unlashed.
With buttons and thread, I start to sew,
A quilt of wishes, let them flow.

Cats prancing by, they take a leap,
Chasing visions that never sleep.
The fabric whispers secrets bright,
While rubber ducks join in the fight.

Laughter echoes, a jumbled scene,
Socks and slippers in shades of green.
As hopes get tangled, they form a crew,
With mismatched colors, they all grew.

In every stitch, a joke unfolds,
A story woven, never old.
With every patch, a giggle shared,
Handcrafted dreams, nobody's scared.

Cross-Stitched Whimsy

Needles dance in a wild ballet,
Stitching giggles throughout the day.
Patterns flow like laughter in air,
Creating chaos, beyond compare.

Hiccups of stitches, they twist and twirl,
As happy thoughts in circles swirl.
A patchwork puppy, a kitten too,
Each one dreams of a sunny hue.

Socks with holes and hats too bright,
Join the fun in a whimsical fight.
Everybody here wears mismatched shoes,
Chasing rainbows, they all amuse.

With every loop, a chuckle grows,
As patterns twist like garden hose.
Embracing life with silly cheer,
In cross-stitch whims, we all adhere.

The Dream Weaver's Song

A weaver hums a tuneful beat,
While socks jump high on tiny feet.
Wool and fabric, they sway with glee,
In a world where fish can climb a tree.

Llamas prance in polka dots,
While knitting needles tie the knots.
A tapestry of jokes and fun,
Under the bright, absurd sun.

Threads of laughter in every hue,
Spin the tales that feel so true.
Buttons roll like bouncy balls,
As fabric claps and joy enthralls.

The weaver's song is wacky, bold,
Spinning tales that never get old.
Each stitch a giggle, every yarn,
In this dance of dreams, we cheer and yarn.

Interwoven Journeys

Once a thread danced in yellow rays,
Chasing shadows in silly ways.
A blanket stitched from funny tales,
With quirks and giggles, it never fails.

Mice in bowties, ducks in shoes,
Joining the party, refusing snooze.
Each journey crossed like paths of fate,
Woven together, never late.

With every twist, a comical cheer,
As socks chat up the chandelier.
Together they plot in playful schemes,
In this stitch of life, we chase our dreams.

So here's to journeys stitched with flair,
Where laughter leaps into the air.
In every loop and every twine,
Life's interwoven yarns combine.

The Knot of Tomorrow's Promise

A shoelace tangled in my shoe,
Promises dangling like morning dew.
I chase a butterfly on the way,
While age-old dreams decide to play.

Socks that never match in pairs,
Which one goes where? No one cares!
A future tied with a ribbon bold,
But it's more like a messy fold.

Cupcakes and confetti in my head,
A circus juggler doing what he said.
The gnome with a hat has a plan to scheme,
Spinning tales of impossible dream.

When laughter stitches through the air,
We rise and tumble without a care.
In this knot of giggles and cheer,
We float as balloons with nothing to fear.

Whispers of Enchantment Through the Threads.

A cat in a hat, oh what a sight,
Whispers of magic in the moonlight.
Yarn rolls away like a sneaky mouse,
My dreams tumble down like a playful house.

The broomsticks dance with pixie dust,
In this cozy corner, oh how I trust.
What's twirled and tangled is how we roam,
Knots and giggles make us feel at home.

With fairies painting our hearts so bright,
We swing from wishes, oh what a flight!
The threads of laughter weave tales so wild,
Every stitch a chuckle, innocent and mild.

In boots that squeak and hats too tall,
We leap through puddles, we rise, we fall.
As shadows whisper with dreamy delight,
We spin with the moon until the sunlight.

Threads of Ambition

A trampoline made of mismatched socks,
Where all the wise owls throw crazy flocks.
With every bounce, my plans take flight,
As gummy worms wiggle in delight.

The ladder to success is made of cheese,
And climbing it brings giggles and wheezes.
While dreams in rubber bands flip and flop,
A parade of marshmallows makes me stop.

Each thread I pull leads to silly places,
Like juggling frogs with make-up faces.
Ambitions dance in a zany waltz,
As jellybeans multiply like they're in a vault.

In a world of fluff, I roam so free,
Mastering art with glee and glee.
While butterflies play hopscotch on my hat,
I chase after joy, imagine that!

Weaving Visions

Through a blender of hopes, I mix and twirl,
My visions fly like a sparkly swirl.
With spaghetti strands tangled in delight,
A muse in a tutu takes off in flight.

The soup of potential bubbles and spins,
Knitted together with laughter that wins.
In the loom of life, we thread with zest,
Each stitch a giggle, a marvelous quest.

Dreams dance like ribbons on windy days,
Happy little suns set in quirky ways.
I knit with gleeful mischief and cheer,
Weaving tales that make the frowns disappear.

As shadows mingle with the radiant light,
Our imaginations weave through day and night.
With each little flip of whimsy we sway,
In the fabric of joy, we laugh and play.

Weft of Wonder

In a land where socks do dance,
They spin around, given the chance.
A rubber duck joins the parade,
Wobbly steps in a sock charade.

Jellybeans bounce on colorful roads,
Each twist and turn lightens our loads.
A trampoline built of dreams and fluff,
Bouncing high, oh, isn't it tough?

A snail in a top hat leads the way,
With a wink, it shouts, "Come, let's play!"
The sun giggles, tickling the sky,
While clouds turn cartwheels way up high.

In this world where giggles are the norm,
Laughter dances, bringing the warm.
Every corner bursts with delight,
Even the shadows join in the fright.

Embroidered Horizons

Stitching stars on a velvet night,
Glittering dreams take off in flight.
A cat in pajamas gives a cheer,
As toast pops out, warm and near.

Balloons float by with goofy grins,
Where every turn, a new tale begins.
Penguins slide on ice cream slides,
While donuts steer their sugary rides.

Mismatched socks start to ballet,
With flip-flops dreaming, they sway.
The moon looks down in a funny hat,
Making wishes where owls sat.

In this patchwork of colors bright,
Giggles weave through the fabric light.
A world of wonder, fun and glee,
Where every stitch tells a tale, you see!

Knots of Curiosity

A curious frog wears a bow tie,
Reading books while the crickets sigh.
With each flip of the page, it croaks,
Sharing stories of silly folks.

Bugs in glasses play chess on leaves,
While ants gossip about oddities and thieves.
A caterpillar contemplates designs,
For a quilt made of pizza fines.

Llamas with hats do silly prances,
Holding court of whimsical lances.
Each tie and twist a story spun,
Of pancake races, oh what fun!

Around the garden, laughter rings,
As butterflies discuss their zany flings.
With each knot, a giggle unfolds,
In a world where chaos is boldly sold.

Web of Intentions

Spiders weave with threads of cheese,
Concocting traps for favorite peas.
Each thread a possibility to explore,
With pepper flakes, they'll dance, then soar.

A squirrel juggles acorns on a whim,
While a raccoon makes bets on a flimsy limb.
Every toss a flicker of light,
As the sun waves in delight.

Bikes with wings fly overhead,
Dodging clouds that look like bread.
Pinecones chime in a beautiful song,
In this land where oddballs belong.

Wrapped in giggles like cozy scarves,
Chasing dreams on silly paths and marves.
In a web where wonders play and spin,
The fun begins, let's dive right in!

Unraveled Futures

In a world of tangled schemes,
Future's thread unravels, it seems.
A sock missing, a shoe in flight,
My plans take off, like birds at night.

Lost my map, but found a hat,
The plan is set! Or just a chat?
Chasing spoons, dodging balloons,
My timeline's full of silly tunes.

With every twist and silly spin,
I laugh and twirl, let chaos win.
A pie on my head, a wink from fate,
Each step ahead feels like a date.

So here we go, off into air,
With a wig on my head, I can't despair.
Futures unraveled, wild and free,
What's next? A dance party by a tree!

Starlit Connections

Oh look! A comet's lost its way,
Zooming by on a dull Monday.
My wishes are trapped in a jar,
Waiting for release, they won't go far.

The stars are chatting, I can hear,
They gossip loud, they spread good cheer.
One wants pizza, another a cake,
All I envisioned was a big mistake.

With every twinkle, I start to grin,
Jumbled constellations, laugh with kin.
As bright as the sun, as silly as a cat,
They poke fun at my mismatched hat.

So smile with me, let's make a wish,
To dance with stars, a cosmic swish.
Connections made through laughter and light,
Starlit chaos in the still of night!

The Fabric of the Mind

A patchwork quilt of thoughts I see,
One square says 'lunch', another 'tea'.
Sewing dreams with spaghetti threads,
Fashioning hats, starchy as breads.

In my head, a jumbled spree,
Thoughts like kittens, purr and flee.
One's knitting sweaters out of cheese,
Hoping to catch a taco breeze.

Pointless ideas often collide,
In two left shoes, I take a ride.
Ideas fray, they twist and knot,
But each is tasty, like a donut pot.

So wear your fabric, funny and bright,
Let's stitch our quirks, what a sight!
The fabric wears smiles, hugs, and quirks,
In our minds, where laughter lurks!

Nurtured Visions

In my garden, ideas sprout,
With roots so funny, can't shake them out.
One wears glasses, another a bow,
Growing wild, as ideas flow.

Watering dreams with fizzy fizzes,
Every petal radiates what blizzards.
Bouncing thoughts like balls of light,
My visions dance, oh what a sight!

A garden party where seeds take flight,
Each one a joke, each one a delight.
With laughter blooming in every space,
Nurtured visions in a funny place.

So let's plant seeds of giggles and cheer,
And watch our dreams burst into the air.
In this wacky world where humor thrives,
Nurtured visions, the funniest lives!

Chasing Shadows

In the park, we run so fast,
Waving hands like crazy at last.
Chasing shadows in the sun,
Laughing hearts, oh what fun!

A squirrel bolts and we both freeze,
Oh look! There's a man with cheese!
We race to catch this cheesy prize,
But trip and tumble, laughter flies!

We build our dreams on sandy shores,
While seagulls steal our crispy scores.
We craft our castles, big and tall,
Only to watch the waves enthrall!

A zany quest, our spirits high,
With silly hats, we soar and fly.
Chasing laughter, hearts so free,
In every moment, just you and me!

Entangled Desires

Two tangled strings on a sunny day,
Try to dance, but they just sway.
In a twist, we trip and fall,
Rolling laughter, oh how we sprawl!

A bee buzzes by, what a surprise,
Chasing after it, we both rise.
With jelly jars on each hand,
We try to catch the buzzing band!

Our dreams are tied with gummy string,
Bouncing high, we feel the spring.
But in our haste, we drop our treats,
A sticky mess, oh the defeats!

Yet through the laughter, we find our way,
In silly antics, we love to play.
With tangled fates, we dance and spin,
In this crazy world, let the fun begin!

Woven Whispers

Whispers float like bubbles in the air,
Spinning tales of jest without a care.
A cat wearing a hat struts down the street,
With every step, it dances to the beat!

Dreams wrapped tight in rainbows bright,
Knotted laughter takes flight in the night.
With mismatched socks, we prance and twirl,
Our silly stories begin to unfurl!

Snagged on a branch, our kite takes a dive,
Flapping wildly, we're trying to thrive.
Yet tangled up in strings of cheer,
Our giggles echo for all to hear!

Through woven whispers, secrets arise,
In this absurd dance, we claim the skies.
With every blink, our antics rise,
A comedy of dreams, with laughter as our prize!

Boundless Threads

A spider spins with threads so fine,
We laugh as we pretend to dine.
On gummy worms and jellybeans,
In this wild feast, you'll hear our screams!

With nimble fingers, we weave and play,
A tapestry of dreams, come what may.
The yarn gets tangled, oops! What a mess,
Yet there's more laughter, I confess!

Jumping around like jolly fools,
We invent our own silly rules.
With every twist, our friendship grows,
In playful chaos, anything goes!

Boundless threads in the fabric of fun,
We're mischievous, shining like the sun.
With every giggle, every cheer,
Life's a mad dance, let's all persevere!

Winding Paths of Desire

I wandered down a crooked lane,
With socks that don't quite match again.
A cat with a hat said, "Don't you see?"
Your dreams are just like my tea — they spill free!

I tripped on a wish, fell flat on my face,
A giggle escaped, oh what a disgrace.
A duck in a bowtie danced with delight,
While clouds did the cha-cha and twinkled at night.

In this wacky world where I'm meant to roam,
A pizza slice promised, "You'll find your home!"
With toppings of laughter, I took a big bite,
And suddenly, the moon was a pizza, alight!

So here's to the journey, the strangeness ahead,
With each twist and turn, we'll laugh till we're dead.
Let's prance through the fields of improbable fun,
In this circus of life, we're always the one!

Constellations of Thought

Stars whispered secrets in playful tones,
While squirrels debated on toasters and groans.
I tangled my thoughts in a very bright mess,
Like ketchup on pancakes, oh what a success!

A comet zoomed by with a flick of its tail,
As I rode a bright rocket that wobbled and frail.
In the galaxy's playground, we swung high and low,
Bouncing on ideas, like jellybeans in tow.

The moon wore a grin, a fabulous sight,
While planets played tag in the soft, starry light.
With dreams in their pockets and giggles galore,
They whispered to me, "There's always much more!"

So let's sketch the skies with our wildest finesse,
Drawing rainbows of nonsense, oh what a success!
In the dance of the cosmos, we'll join hand in hand,
And paint our confusions in glittering sand!

The Knitting of Potential

In a land where the yarn thrived, oh so bright,
A turtle knitted socks that fit just right.
With needles that sparkled and patterns so grand,
She created a scarf that tickled the hand!

Each loop held a giggle, a chuckle, a cheer,
As colors danced wildly, releasing all fear.
"Let's stitch up the sunsets, the moonbeams, the smiles,"
Said the rabbit who knitted with fabulously wild styles.

From glimmers of sunlight to concepts of fun,
The yarn spun ideas that sparked everyone.
With each twist and turn, our thoughts interweave,
Like spaghetti on forks, oh what a reprieve!

So come grab a needle, join in on the fun,
In the knitting of potential, all can be done!
With laughter and colors, we'll share in the glee,
Creating a tapestry of who we can be!

Knots of Serendipity

Tangled up in a colorful spree,
A jester danced wildly, swinging from a tree.
With every odd knot, a new tale would grow,
As laughter unraveled in the midst of the show.

A penguin in slippers googled for fun,
While bananas and apples discussed who had won.
Chasing their tails, they spun round and round,
In this curious world where silliness found!

With a yarn ball of giggles, rolled under my bed,
I tripped over wishes that danced in my head.
The more that I stumbled, the more I would find,
Each knot a surprise, each twist was so kind!

So here's to the chaos, the laughs that ensue,
In the knots of chance where the funny shines through.
Navigating the maze with a smile (and a grin),
Let's embrace the absurdity swirling within!

Sacred Twine

In a world of fuzzy yarn,
Kittens chase and rainbows yarn,
Every knot a giggle brings,
Lopsided hats that dance and sing.

Twist and turn, a slippery slide,
Giggles bounce, we cannot hide,
Dreams get tangled in a ball,
Roll with laughter, have a ball.

With each loop, a playful twist,
Wobbly stitches none could miss,
Giant squirrels knit in the trees,
Whispers float on gentle breeze.

In this maze of colored thread,
Chasing thoughts, but none to dread,
We weave a world filled with cheer,
Juggling joy all through the year.

The Patchwork Path

On the road, a patchwork trail,
Flapping clothes tell their own tale,
A sock that sings, a vest that hops,
Each step brings laughter, never stops.

Quilts of dreams stitch far and wide,
Funky patterns, a silly ride,
We skip and jump, a dance with glee,
Belly laughs and butterflies flee.

Threaded paths of joy and fun,
Sunshine giggles, moonlight run,
Every corner holds a jest,
Ticklish journeys, never rest.

With every patch, a tale unfolds,
Wacky stories, laughter bold,
Join the parade, come take a chance,
In the silly, we all can prance.

Dreams Entwined

Snakes in pajamas, wiggle and worm,
Dancing dreams, they twist and squirm,
Hat made of gumdrops, shoes of cheese,
Wearing smiles, with effortless ease.

Whimsical wishes fly with flair,
Twirling thoughts in the jelly air,
Banana peels and sprinkles bright,
Chasing giggles into the night.

Lions do the limbo, owls wear hats,
Bouncing beagles, and elastic cats,
Every thought, a silly game,
In this world, none are the same.

Laughs wrapped in a silly disguise,
Catch the joy before it flies,
With dreams entwined, we leap and bound,
In the circus of joy, we're all around.

Harmony in Chaos

In a world where socks all run,
Frogs wear crowns, and dance for fun,
Jesters juggle, pie on their face,
Every mistake a silly grace.

Cat on a skateboard, watch it glide,
Riding dreams, evolving the ride,
Chaos reigns but here's the twist,
Laughter's the prize, it can't be missed.

Bouncing bubbles, tickle the air,
Whirling wonders, everywhere,
In this mess, we find a tune,
A serenade beneath the moon.

Dreamers dashing in funky shoes,
Creating laughter, nothing to lose,
In the chaos, joy's a must,
Embracing whimsy, oh, what a trust.

Intertwined in the Dance of Expectations

In a world where plans take flight,
Each step is a leap, a quirky delight.
We dance with hope, a silly pirouette,
Tripping on laughter, a joy to beget.

Twists like spaghetti, oh what a sight,
Partners in chaos, a comical plight.
A tango of wishes, lost in the breeze,
With every misstep, we laugh with ease.

Balloons in the air, our dreams take a twirl,
Chasing after giggles, each twist makes us whirl.
In this madcap ballet, we stumble and sigh,
Yet, oh how we shimmer, like stars in the sky.

So here's to the dance, though tangled we are,
Creating a ruckus, we shine like a star.
With dreams intertwined, it's chaos we flaunt,
In the jig of our journey, we laugh and we haunt.

The Mosaic of Wishes

A patchwork of thoughts in a colorful mess,
Dreams on a canvas, no time to digress.
Bold strokes of laughter, splashes of cheer,
In a gallery of hope, we hold what is dear.

Some wishes are giant, some fit in a frame,
A pinwheel of hope, they swirl in a game.
From silly to serious, we paint with a grin,
Each brushstroke of chaos, a reason to spin.

With crayon-colored laughter, we scribble our fate,
Each doodle a reminder not to hesitate.
Like jigsaw puzzles glued with our dreams,
We laugh at the chaos, however it seems.

In this vibrant mosaic, we join hand in hand,
Crafting our wishes, a whimsical band.
So here's to our journey, a crazy parade,
Where dreams become colors, no chance to fade.

Ensnared by Inspiration

Caught in the web of a wild idea,
Giggles erupt, as we twist and we leer.
Chasing our thoughts like bubbles in the air,
Every whim dances, a mischievous dare.

With socks on our hands, we strut down the street,
Inspiration tugs at the shoelaces of feet.
A parade of oddities, all giggles and glee,
In this circus of madness, we are truly free.

Ideas take flight on a banana peel glide,
Each slip is an adventure, with laughter as our guide.
We juggle our dreams, both funny and bright,
In the chaos of creation, we find our delight.

So let the inspiration ensnare us today,
With whimsies so grand, we'll merrily play.
In this circus of life, we'll swing from the beams,
And dance in the glow of our outlandish dreams.

Frayed Edges of Anticipation

Anticipation swirls like a kite in the breeze,
With frayed edges fluttering, a tease that appease.
Each moment a giggle, a twinkle in sight,
Hoping for tomorrow, with a wink of delight.

Our hats are a jumble, our shoes mismatched,
Every tick of the clock, our excitement dispatched.
We countdown like children, with glee in our hearts,
Each second a puzzle, a whimsical art.

Thoughts flit around like fireflies at night,
Chasing the glow of what feels just right.
Our dreams are a riddle, all tangled yet clear,
With laughter as music, we dance without fear.

So let the frayed edges lead us astray,
Embracing the chaos, come what may.
In the laughter of waiting, we find our own way,
With the whims of our heart, in joy we will stay.

Knotted Paths of Imagination

Bouncing thoughts like rubber balls,
In a world where logic stalls,
Twisted paths in wacky ways,
Chasing dreams through funky maze.

Laughter echoes, giggles burst,
As silly ideas take their first,
Jumping jacks of fanciful schemes,
Weaving laughter from our dreams.

Noodles dance on spaghetti strings,
While talking cats play with their flings,
A circus full of clowns and cheers,
Imagined fun that lasts for years.

So grab your hat, let's take a ride,
On knotted paths where joys reside,
We'll stitch our silly visions bright,
And float on laughter's pure delight.

Stitches of the Soul's Desires

In a sewing room of wishes spun,
Buttons laugh and thread has fun,
Needles poke at daily dread,
Crafting joy with every thread.

Patchwork hearts and mismatched socks,
Whiskered cats that synonymize clocks,
Stitch by stitch, our hopes will gleam,
In a quilted tapestry of a dream.

Threads entwined in a dance so grand,
Silly patterns we've unplanned,
With every laugh, we stitch away,
Creating joy in a quirky way.

So bring your fabrics, bright and bold,
Together we'll make laughter gold,
With every stitch, our hearts align,
In a humor-filled design divine.

Echoes of a Dreamer's Loom

In a loom where dreams collide,
A jester's hat on the side,
Woolen whispers, bright and loud,
Crafting chaos in a shroud.

Dancing fibers spin and sway,
Tangled thoughts come out to play,
Weaving laughter in every seam,
Fabricating the perfect dream.

Wobbly stitches, bright and fun,
Links of glee that can't be outrun,
From fuzzy yarns to silky strands,
We'll knit our laughter with our hands.

So grab your spindle, join the song,
In this loom, you can't go wrong,
Echoes of joy, let them bloom,
In a colorful, crazy room.

The Interlace of Heartfelt Visions

From the depths of a crooked mind,
Ideas whirl like leaves unconfined,
In a jigsaw puzzle made of dreams,
Colors clash, or so it seems.

Crayon skies and jellybean trees,
Oh, the taste of funny cheese,
Crafting giggles with a twist,
In a world where smiles persist.

Frogs in top hats dance and laugh,
As we scribble our goofy graph,
Binding joy in every play,
With witty words that shout "hooray!"

So gather round, let visions blend,
In this whimsically fun trend,
We'll interlace with mirthful cheers,
And stitch our laughter through the years.

Spheres of Inspiration

In a world where thoughts take flight,
Balloons filled with giggles, oh what a sight!
They bob and weave, in playful dance,
Caught on the wind, they twist and prance.

A cat in a hat, chasing dreams so bold,
With each little leap, more stories unfold.
A pie on a tree, what a curious feat,
Sharing sweet wishes, can't be beat!

Chasing the stars with a hop and a skip,
Tap dancing wishes on a chocolate chip.
Laughter erupts as they soar and zing,
In the land of ideas, joy's the real king.

So grab a balloon, come join the parade,
In this silliness, no one is afraid.
With each wobbly giggle and carefree cheer,
The spheres of wonder forever draw near.

Anchored Wishes

A boat made of marshmallows, afloat on a whim,
Sets sail on a river, where dreams start to brim.
With candy cane anchors, they hold steady tight,
While jellybean fish play hide and seek in the light.

A pickle on deck, wearing captain's attire,
Yells 'Set the sails!' with a voice full of fire.
The crew of gumdrops, all ready to go,
In this sugary sea, just follow the flow.

On waves of pure frosting, they giggle and glide,
With laughter and cream, they float side by side.
From island to island, their wishes take flight,
Each moment a treasure, a spark of delight.

At dusk, when the skies turn a peachy soft hue,
They gather round fires, with stories anew.
Anchored in joy, on this whimsical ride,
Their silly adventures make hearts swell with pride.

Boundless Horizons

A kite filled with laughter, bursts into the blue,
With candy-coated wishes, dancing and true.
It flips and it flutters, oh what a game,
Tugging at dreams like they're all just the same.

In fields of confetti, we run wild and free,
Chasing the moments as they giggle with glee.
A rabbit in pajamas hops over the grass,
In this land of wonder, time seems to pass.

With twinkling lights strung on a cotton candy moon,
We laugh with the stars, our hearts out of tune.
Each horizon a canvas, painted with cheer,
As silly balloon characters draw us all near.

We'll build our own castles with wishes, not sand,
With each silly moment, together we stand.
Boundless and bright, with joy as our guide,
In the land of imagination, we will abide.

The Threaded Odyssey

A shoelace of giggles leads on to the quest,
Where hiccups and snorts turn into a jest.
We spin tales of yarn, with laughter entwined,
In this quirky adventure, all joy is designed.

Through forests of sprinkles and rivers of jam,
We sail on a raft made from fresh peanut bam.
Each twist of the thread reveals stories to share,
As wiggly worms host a dance in the air.

A squirrel in a tutu, with moves like no other,
Swoops in with a joke, like an old goofy brother.
With stitches of kindness we weave our own fate,
Laughing out loud, there's no room for hate.

So come join the voyage, with smiles in the breeze,
As we journey together, with hearts full of ease.
In the threaded odyssey, we'll find our delight,
For laughter's the compass that guides through the night.

Knots of Ambition

I tied my socks, they never matched,
Their colors clash, a fashion snatched.
I dream of gold, but found old boots,
With laces tangled, I laugh, who hoots?

A tie, a bow, a slipknot done,
My future looks just like this pun.
I chase the stars, but trip on air,
My path's a circus, full of flair.

I built tall towers, with blocks of cheer,
But they tumble down—oh dear, oh dear!
Each block a wish, they spiral high,
One silly leap, and whoosh, I fly!

In this tangled mess, my giggles bloom,
Ambition's dance finds space in gloom.
With every knot, I clap and cheer,
The laughter's loud, my path is clear!

Weaving Night's Whispers

With threads of starlight, I weave my tale,
A tapestry bright with dreams that sail.
My cat's my muse, she pounces with glee,
She snags my yarn, oh where could it be?

I whisper wishes to the midnight sky,
While drinking tea with a giggling spy.
We stitch the moon with laughter loud,
And dance like fairies in a funny crowd.

I shout to the stars, "Join my parade!"
But they twinkle back, "We're not afraid!"
Each wish a stitch, in this cosmic quilt,
With all the laughter, my fears are spilt.

A chorus of dreams, they jig and jive,
In every fiber, my hopes arrive.
With night's own whispers, my heart takes flight,
In this woven world, I laugh all night.

Threads of Unseen Aspirations

With threads unseen, I plot my game,
In every wink, there's no one to blame.
A needle that laughs, it stitches tight,
As aspirations twirl in a comical flight.

I aim for the stars, but fall in the mud,
With dreams all messy, it's quite a thud!
Each laugh a knot that holds me steady,
I grow my hopes, but stay unready.

A ball of yarn in my zestful clutch,
My plans unwind, it's all too much.
I chase the sun, but it runs away,
A funny little game we both play.

Yet in this twist, I find the cheer,
Each dream a joke that draws me near.
With threads of laughter, I stitch my fate,
In unseen hopes, I celebrate!

A Tapestry of Moonlit Wishes

In moonlit glow, I weave my fables,
With giggles mixed in fairytales' stables.
Each wish a patch, some odd and bright,
They dance around, a silly sight.

I stitched a cow to leaping dreams,
It jumped so high, it burst at the seams!
A patchwork quilt of jests and rhymes,
With every loop, I laugh at time.

My dreams are hats, all tall and wide,
With flying fish and a kangaroo ride.
They flutter mad like butterflies,
With every whim, my spirit flies.

In this tapestry, I find my bliss,
With every laugh, there's magic kissed.
In moonlit wishes, a world unfurls,
Where silly dreams create such swirls.

Threads of Elysium

In the land where socks go astray,
A realm where rubber bands love to play.
Unicorns fly on jello-like beams,
While marshmallows spin in candy-filled dreams.

Lollipop trees sway with a grin,
As giggling gnomes bring the mischief within.
Silly hats dance in the sticky sweet sun,
A festival of laughter, oh what fun!

Kites made of cupcakes soar through the skies,
With sprinkles of laughter and joyous surprise.
In Elysium's heart where the weird collides,
We weave silly dreams as the laughter abides.

So grab a balloon and let's twirl around,
In this wacky world where giggles abound.
Every step taken, a frolicsome chance,
In the threads of Elysium, let's dance, dance, dance!

Cascading Fantasies

A waterfall of jelly glistens bright,
With penguins skating, oh what a sight!
In this world where bananas wear hats,
And kangaroos play chess with chitchatting cats.

Marshmallow clouds float on cotton candy,
Where silly rabbits think they're quite dandy.
Riding bicycles made out of cheese,
Each wobble and giggle sets hearts at ease.

Ticklish toasters pop up with cheer,
Spitting out toast when our friends are near.
In a stream of hiccups and whimsical sighs,
We surf on the smiles that freely arise.

Cascading dreams swirl and twist on parade,
With a sprinkle of laughter, let fun never fade.
Join us in folly, let worries take flight,
In a world full of whimsy, everything's bright!

The Cartographer's Dream

Maps made of pizza, what a delight,
With pepperoni mountains scaling to new height.
Every cheesy corner holds a treasure or two,
And rivers of soda that bubble and brew.

A compass that spins like a fidgeting friend,
This crazy adventure will never end.
With marshmallow forests and gumdrop roads,
Our cartographer dances, and giggles explode.

Navigating wonderlands filled with smiles,
Through paths paved with cupcakes that stretch for miles.
In this land of whimsy, let laughter be seen,
Drawing the laughter on each page pristine.

So grab your crayons, let's sketch out this quest,
In the cartographer's dream, let's be our best!
With maps full of chuckles, we'll wander and roam,
In a topsy-turvy world, together we'll comb!

Unbreakable Bonds

Two silly squirrels tied with a string,
Dance down the lane, oh what joy they bring.
With acorn hats and giggling fills,
They share the laughter and playful thrills.

Jumping on pogo sticks made of cake,
Creating a ruckus with each little shake.
In this bond of humor, they twine and twist,
Spreading joy that can never be missed.

A rubber chicken shrieks, oh how it squeals,
As they weave through the forest, sharing big meals.
With marshmallow mates, their friendship expands,
Unbreakable bonds tie them hand in hand.

So let's laugh like these squirrels, for life's a big jest,
With sprinkles of joy, we'll always be blessed.
In our whimsical world, let laughter resound,
In unbreakable bonds, true joy can be found!

The Loom of Tomorrow

In a land where wishes dance,
They prance and twirl in merry chance.
With every thought, a thread we weave,
A tapestry of laughs, we conceive.

Socks that fly, and cats that sing,
Chasing shadows of imaginary spring.
We knit the sun with a wink and grin,
In this wacky world, where chuckles begin.

Frogs in top hats, sipping tea,
Juggling dreams under a lemon tree.
The clouds wear shoes and strut about,
In this oddball tale, there's never a doubt.

With every giggle, a color spark,
In the loom of tomorrow, we leave a mark.
So grab a laugh, and spin the fun,
Together we'll craft, until we're done.

Interlaced Fantasies

In a circus of thoughts, we jump and fly,
A jester's cap and a wink in the eye.
Pies in the sky and dreams on a spoon,
Laughter erupts like a joyful balloon.

Balloons that pop with a silly cheer,
Tickling the toes of the passing deer.
Spinning tales in a wild parade,
With each funny line, an escapade.

Socks that melt into puddles of glee,
Whiskers on fish sipping herbal tea.
We spin the yarn, and the chaos ensues,
In the world of the absurd, we can't lose.

Giggles and snuggles, a hearty embrace,
Every quirk adds to this wild space.
In interlaced fantasies, we find our art,
With laughter as fabric, it warms the heart.

The Art of Connection

A banana phone rings in the night,
Chasing thoughts that take flight.
Wizards in pajamas sipping hot cocoa,
Juggling jellybeans in a joyous show.

Puppies doodling on charred old maps,
While singing fish make silly claps.
Connecting worlds on a trampoline,
In a sketchbook where nonsense reigns supreme.

Kites made of pizza, flying so high,
Chasing clouds that wave goodbye.
Every chuckle a stepping stone,
Creating bonds in the wacky unknown.

With each punchline, a rainbow appears,
Weaving laughter through the space of years.
The art of connection, hilariously grand,
A masterpiece drawn by a laughing hand.

Embracing Possibilities

A pickle parade down a candy lane,
Bouncing clouds on a sugar train.
Silly hats and mismatched shoes,
In the realm of whimsy, we can't lose.

Dancing to the sound of bubbling tea,
While marshmallows sprinkle across the sea.
Butterflies wearing glasses and ties,
Flapping joy in the sunny skies.

With every giggle, the world expands,
Turning planters into marching bands.
Embracing the absurd, we spin in delight,
Creating adventures that take off in flight.

So grab your dreams and let them whirl,
In this carnival of imagination's pearl.
With giggles and grins, we'll make a stand,
Embracing possibilities across this land.

Knots of Hope

In a garden of whims, where wishes swing,
My shoelaces dance like they own the spring.
A cat in a hat, with a dream to adopt,
Laughs with a dog, 'til the day they flop.

Tangled and twisty, the yarns of delight,
We knit silly patterns even in the night.
A fish on a bike, what a sight to behold,
Waving their fins, their stories unfold.

When socks start to chatter about plans to collide,
With tacos in tow, they take to the ride.
Through rainbows and giggles, they whirl and they spin,
Each twist is a tale, where silliness wins.

So if you feel lost and you're in a weird jam,
Just follow the laughter, it leads to the bam!
Knots of affection, all silly and bright,
Dance with your dreams, you'll laugh through the night.

Stitched Together

A patchwork of laughter is sewn with surprise,
Where whacky ideas pop up and rise.
Two spoons in a dance, they wiggle and sway,
While wearing odd socks on a fine holiday.

With buttons like balloons that float in a cheer,
The needle slips in, stitching joy near.
A fish on a skateboard, sporting a grin,
In this quilt of life, laughter's the win.

When cupcakes decide to have a parade,
They march with sprinkles, unafraid!
A merry-go-round with socks that can sing,
Life's even better when you twirl in a swing.

So gather your laughter, let's roll up our sleeves,
We'll weave silly stories till everyone leaves.
With threads full of giggles and patches of mirth,
We craft our adventures with boundless worth.

Fabric of Aspirations

In the loom of the cosmos, where dreams are spun,
A chicken in trousers claims it's all just fun.
While rugs with ambitions twirl with delight,
Making it dance through the glimmering night.

The sheets in the corner listen in glee,
As socks tell their tales of what they can be.
With tapestries woven of wishes and sighs,
They dream of the day when they'll reach for the skies.

With buttons as stars and thread as the light,
Each stitch holds a secret, oh what a sight!
A unicorn joins in, wearing a bow,
Sprinkling giggles wherever they go.

So grab your old quilt and wrap up your fun,
In the fabric of laughter, freedom's begun.
With each silly tear, and each joke that we weave,
We'll dream side by side, oh how we believe!

Bound by Wishes

In a land where the cupcakes rule by decree,
They dance with the jellies, so wild and free.
With wishes like balloons, they float in the breeze,
Whispering secrets with sugary ease.

A frog in a bowtie and shoes two sizes too big,
Croaks out a tune while he does a spill jig.
Together they leap, in synchrony they prance,
With stars in their eyes, they lead the mad dance.

As marbles collide in a colorful clash,
The dreams in their pockets begin to splash.
With wishes unfurled in a wild parade,
They paint every moment and never evade.

So come join this party, there's room for us all,
We'll giggle and wiggle and have ourselves a ball.
Bound with our laughter, let the good times flow,
In a world where our wishes together can grow.

www.ingramcontent.com/pod-product-compliance
Lightning Source LLC
Chambersburg PA
CBHW070003300426
43661CB00141B/162